WHY DO I
SLEEP?

BY Emilie Dufresne

BookLife
PUBLISHING

©2019
BookLife Publishing Ltd.
King's Lynn
Norfolk PE30 4LS

All rights reserved.
Printed in Malaysia.

A catalogue record for this
book is available from the
British Library.

ISBN: 978-1-78637-569-8

Written by:
Emilie Dufresne

Edited by:
John Wood

Designed by:
Danielle Rippengill

Image Credits

All images are courtesy of Shutterstock.com, unless otherwise specified. With thanks to Getty Images, Thinkstock Photo and iStockphoto. Front Cover & 1 – Dmitry Natashin, Nadzin, Iconic Bestiary, Vivid vector. Images used on every spread – Nadzin, TheFarAwayKingdom. 2–4 – Iconic Bestiary. 6 – svtdesign. 7 – Iconic Bestiary. 8 – derter. 9 – eHrach, Iconic Bestiary. 10–16 – Iconic Bestiary. 17 – Roi and Roi. 18–19 – Iconic Bestiary. 20 – Perfect Vectors. 21 – HedgehogVector. 22&23 – Iconic Bestiary. 23 – Perfect Vectors.

CONTENTS

Words that look like **this** can be found in the glossary on page 24.

Are You Feeling Tired?

Is it getting late? Are you feeling sleepy and want to go to bed? Most people get tired in the evenings.

It looks like you need a good night's rest!

All through the day, our bodies and minds have lots of important jobs to do, such as using our **muscles** or learning new things. That's a lot of work!

Sleep lets us recharge our bodies and lets our brain sort out all the information.

Yawning

Sometimes we yawn when we are tired and sleepy. Scientists aren't exactly sure why we yawn. At first, they thought it was to get more **oxygen** into our bodies, but this wasn't true.

LUNGS

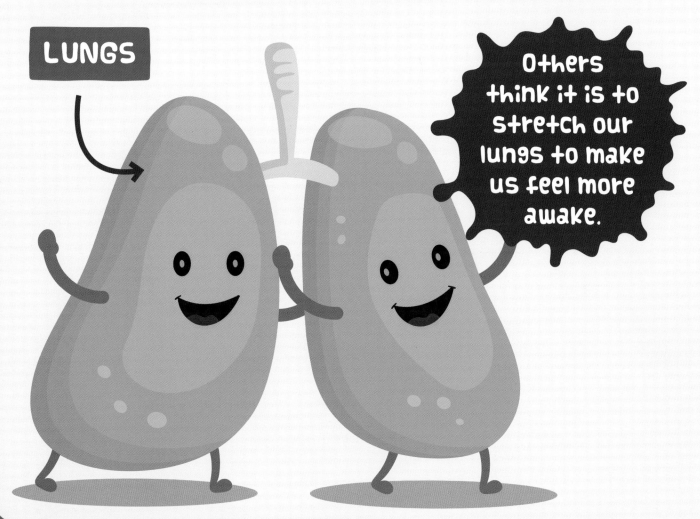

Others think it is to stretch our lungs to make us feel more awake.

Have you ever noticed that yawns are catching? When one person yawns, a person near them will probably yawn too.

Nobody really knows why yawns are catching – but you want to yawn right now, don't you?

Going to Bed

There are certain things you can do before you even get into bed to help you get a better night's sleep. Here are a few examples.

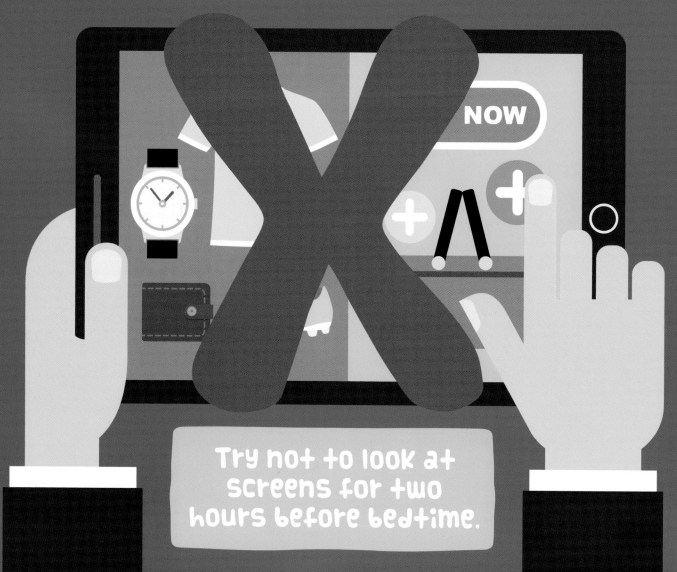

Try not to look at screens for two hours before bedtime.

Have a warm, relaxing bath before bed.

Keep your bedroom dark and quiet.

All these things should help you have a long and peaceful night's sleep.

Sleep Phases

As you sleep, you go through lots of different phases.

PHASE 1:

You are barely asleep and can easily wake up, sometimes with a **SUDDEN JERK**. Your eyes may be slightly open.

PHASE 2:

This is a slightly deeper phase of sleep and your body <u>temperature</u> begins to drop.

PHASE 3:

This is the deepest phase of sleep. It is when the body **repairs** and **GROWS**, while also strengthening the <u>immune system</u>.

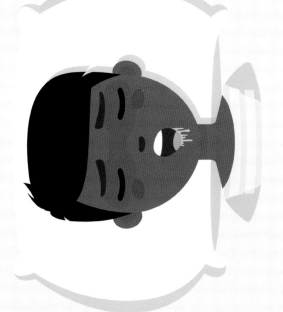

PHASE 4:

This phase of sleep is known as Rapid Eye Movement sleep (REM). This is when you have **vivid** dreams or nightmares.

The different stages of sleep can come in different orders at different times of the night.

Snoring and Dribbling

Sometimes when we sleep, we can dribble all over our pillows.

Our bodies are always making saliva (spit). When awake, we just swallow the saliva. But when we are asleep, the muscles in our face relax and the saliva leaks out.

Snoring also happens because our facial muscles are relaxed. Sometimes your mouth, throat, and airways in your nose can **vibrate** as you breathe.

ZZZz

zzzZZ

This can make very loud noises as you breathe in and out!

Dreams

We mostly dream in phase four of sleep. Our brains almost act as if we are awake, but without our bodies moving.

Most of the time we won't remember a dream unless we are woken up in the middle of it.

Nightmares

Nightmares are dreams that might scare us or wake us up screaming or sweating. Don't worry! Everyone will have nightmares at some point in their life.

Scientists think we have nightmares because of evolution. They helped us to be ready for any scary things out there!

We can have nightmares about lots of different things. Sometimes they might be about things that are happening in real life.

Other times they might be about imaginary things such as zombies or monsters!

Sleepwalking

When a sleeping person walks around or acts as if they are still awake, it is called sleepwalking. Sleepwalking usually takes place in phase three of sleep, and can include talking or walking about.

It may seem scary, but sleepwalking is completely normal.

If you see someone sleepwalking, it is important not to startle them. Make them feel safe and try and lead them back to bed.

Usually, people grow out of sleepwalking.

Wetting the Bed

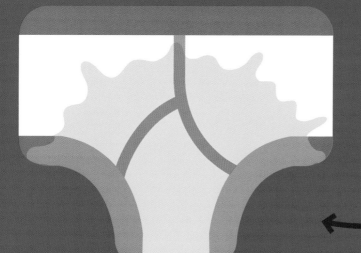

Sometimes we can wet the bed. This can happen in phase three of sleep.

We might be so deeply asleep that we don't realise we need a wee – and we might even dream we are going to the toilet!

If you often wet the bed, try not to drink water an hour before bedtime and make sure you have a wee before going to bed.

Don't worry; children usually grow out of bedwetting.

Sleepy Stats

Five minutes after waking up, you will have forgotten around half of your dream. →

Humans can spend up to a third of their lives asleep.

Activity

Can you match the picture to the right phase of sleep?
Check back through the book if you can't remember.

A.

B.

C.

D.

Answers: A. Stage 3, B. Stage 3, C. Stage 4, D. Stage 1

Glossary

evolution	the process by which living things develop over time
immune system	the system that our body uses to defend itself against illness
muscles	bundles of tissue that can contract or squeeze together
oxygen	a natural gas that most living things need in order to survive
repairs	fixes or mends
temperature	how hot or cold something is
vibrate	to move up and down, left and right or back and forward very fast
vivid	clear or bright

Index